THE
SEED
OF
A
SLAVE

Our Seeds Were
Born For Greatness

IRENE BOOKER

DEDICATION

This keepsake is dedicated

to our ancestors

who marched and died,

in order for us, to live the life,

they could only dream of.

Their prayers and sacrifices

should never be forgotten.

Their strength in unison

should be a reflection

of each of us today.

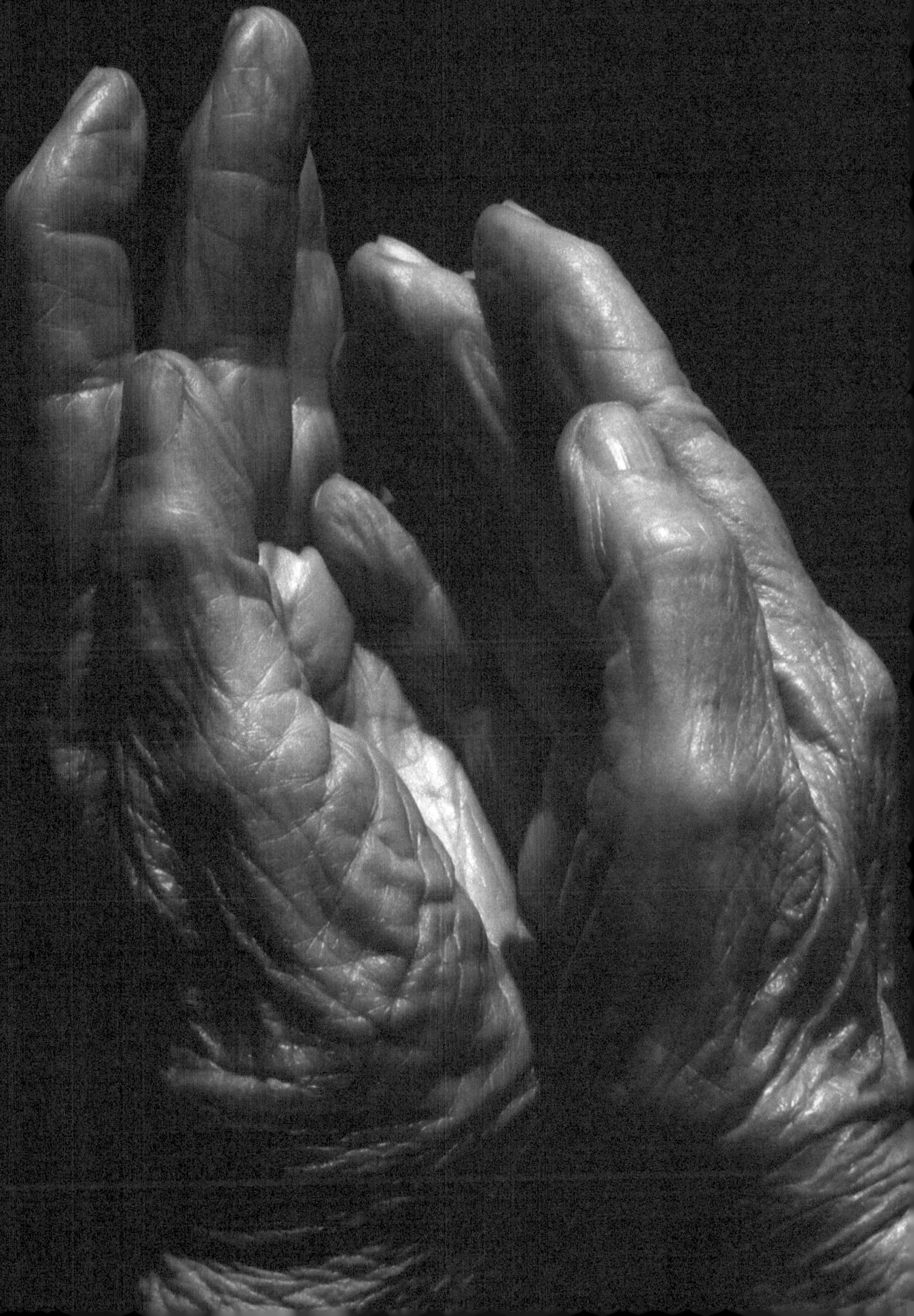

Our great, great, grandfathers paved the way,

Our great, great, grandmothers prayed for a better day.

A seed created from love filled the skies,

A new born slave cries.

Brothers sold as their mom weep,

Staring at her newborn as he sleep.

His fate determined before his birth,

His mother mourns his life,

aware of the pain, the hurt.

His daddy sold before his birth,

Never to know his son, his wife gave birth.

His seed travel with no connection,

Generations lost, searching for their father's affection.

When the dream dies, hope dies.

Look into your mirror and ask yourself,

would our ancestors be ashamed of the dream

that died each time a black baby cried.

I often think of the sacrifices our ancestors made.

Wandering, if a lot of us truly understand

what it means to give your life

for the seeds of our future generations.

Somewhere along the way,

the unity in our traditions were lost.

The love and the respect have been lost.

How can we get back to where we once were,

when unity stood as power?

Our greatness has been evaporated by ignorance.

We are ignorant to the ways of our ancestors.

The seeds of our ancestors are lost in translation.

We must find our way back to our beginning

and our ever florescent past.

Today, we live in a world,

that our ancestors could only have prayed for.

We take for granted, the roads which were paved for us.

Our ancestors died for our freedom.

A lot of us take our lives for granted.

We allow ignorance to blind us from our greatness.

Our seeds were born for greatness,

not less than, not to settle, not to make excuses.

There is no reason, why, we cannot strive each day

of our life to have what all other nationalities have.

There is no excuse!

We're not living on the master's plantation,

but we are still paying the master's house notes.

We are not being put in chains,

and sold from plantation to plantation,

but we are abusing our bodies

taking their drugs,

encompassing one dependency after another.

You're selling yourselves for them!

Here we are today,

shopping at all of the stores

within our neighborhood

and outside of our neighborhoods,

only to realize one thing -

when does the cycle of dependency end?

Our ancestors bought their goods,

from the plantation owners within their reach.

They did not have the choices that you and I have today.

Keep in mind, we have choices,

but again we are ignorant to the ways of our ancestors.

Therefore, we settle for what is in front of us,

rather than creating our own.

Our brains are asleep, while we lie awake.

When one seed thrive, another seed is nourished,

in order for another seed to follow. Sow the seed!

We have to re-educate our minds to our greatness.

Our ancestors knew the power in unity,

we on the other hand,

have become ignorant to the ways of our past and our future.

Elevate your mind, nourish the seed,

ignorance beget ignorance, not power.

There has been a great injustice to our ancestors,

when we allow stupidity to rule our minds.

We have welcomed ignorance into our homes.

We have allowed stupidity to rule our household.

We are raising our seeds when we are mentally asleep.

We have allowed dependencies to cripple our dinner table.

Our ancestors wore chains around their necks,

today, we wear chains around our brains.

We are mentally handicap to the ways of this world.

Our ancestors, faced every atrocity known to man

and yet their seeds walk like zombies,

in this land known too well for their history.

Awaken the seed, stimulate your brain,

connect to the teachings of our ancestors.

Learn your history and educate yourselves!

Remember the book that comforted our ancestors,

remember the book that so many died trying to read,

that book is available today.

Read it, study it,

read every book that will stimulate your brain and fuel your soul.

If there is a secret in it, find it, study it and master it.

Re-educate yourselves and awaken the seed within you.

Tell yourselves daily, we were born for greatness, not less than.

Our ancestors paved the way.

The fruits of their labor must not be in vain.

Each of us have to re-ignite the dream,

the dream is bigger than any of us could have ever imagined.

That's why, we their seeds, can never settle.

We have become financially handicap to a system of dependency.

Mentally, your mind is a slave to the finances of this world.

There was a time, when our ancestors were not allowed to own

currency, therefore, they had no way of bargaining

for goods and services.

Today, a lot of us welcome dependency

on a system that robs you of your independence.

You have become slaves to a financial system

that handicaps your self-respect.

Your greatness should never be sold for a monthly stipend.

Our ancestors were sold,

today, you sell your souls.

Suffocate the brain, kill the spirit,

in return, you murder the seed.

During slavery,

we stood in unison.

Today, we are

divided by ignorance

and led by stupidity.

We are the seed of our ancestors.

Awaken your consciousness to our greatness.

Teach your offsprings of their self-worth.

Awaken a forgotten nation of people.

We breath the air, our ancestors laid down their lives for.

The labor of
our ancestors.

www.ingramcontent.com/pod-product-compliance
Lightning Source LLC
Chambersburg PA
CBHW060829290526
45792CB00005BB/1851